We're going to have a baby!
Our baby is already here.
Baby is hiding inside Mum's belly,
You'll meet baby within a year.

Mum and Dad made baby with love,
With love, baby will continue to grow.
Into our precious youngest one,
But the process is long and slow.

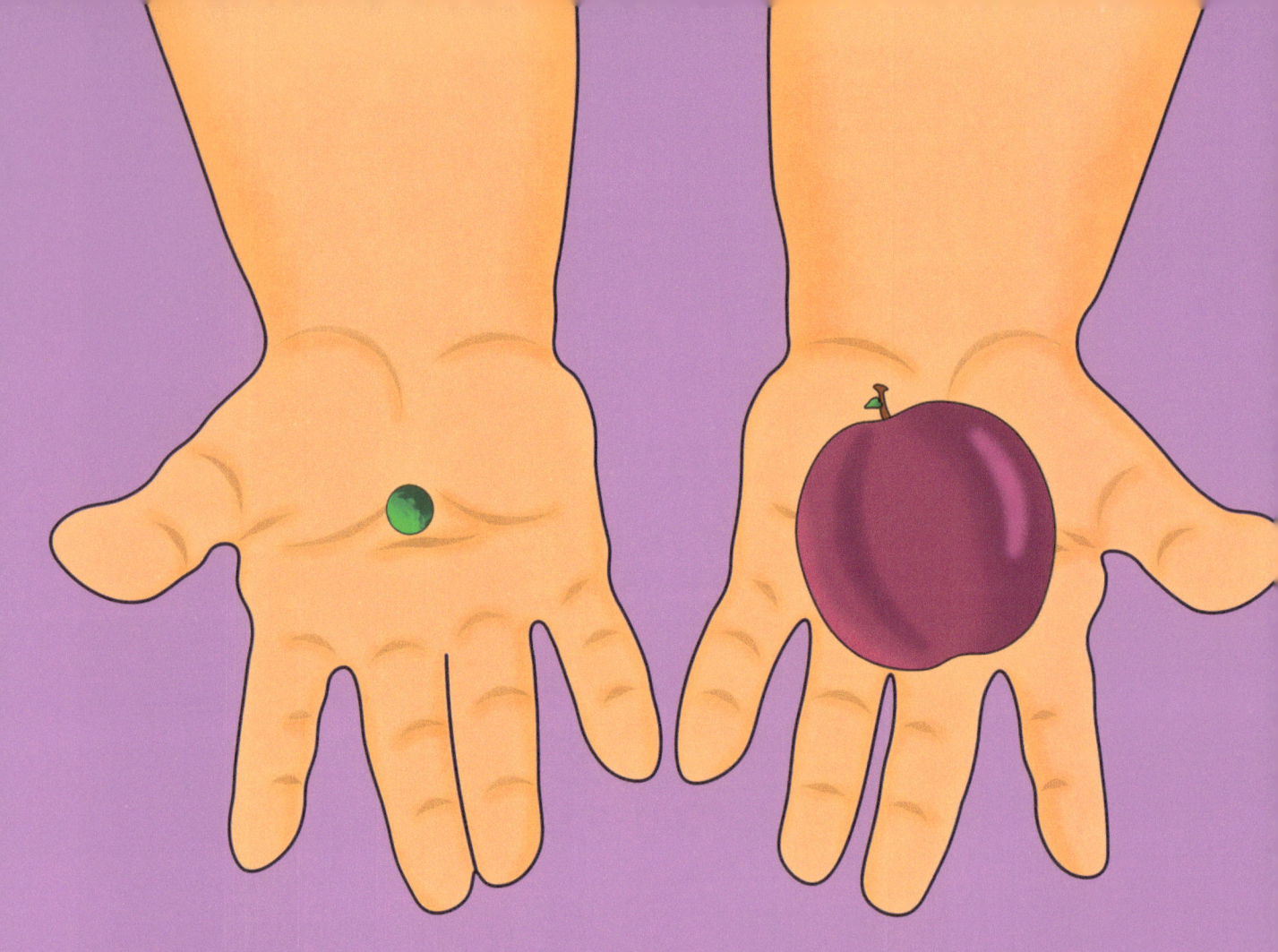

Baby was once smaller than a pea,
And is now the size of a plum.
Baby is growing by the week,
So is Mum's belly bump.

Touch Mum's belly with your hand and cheek
Sing and speak to your special pal.
Soon you will feel baby roll and kick,
Baby will listen to all you have to tell.

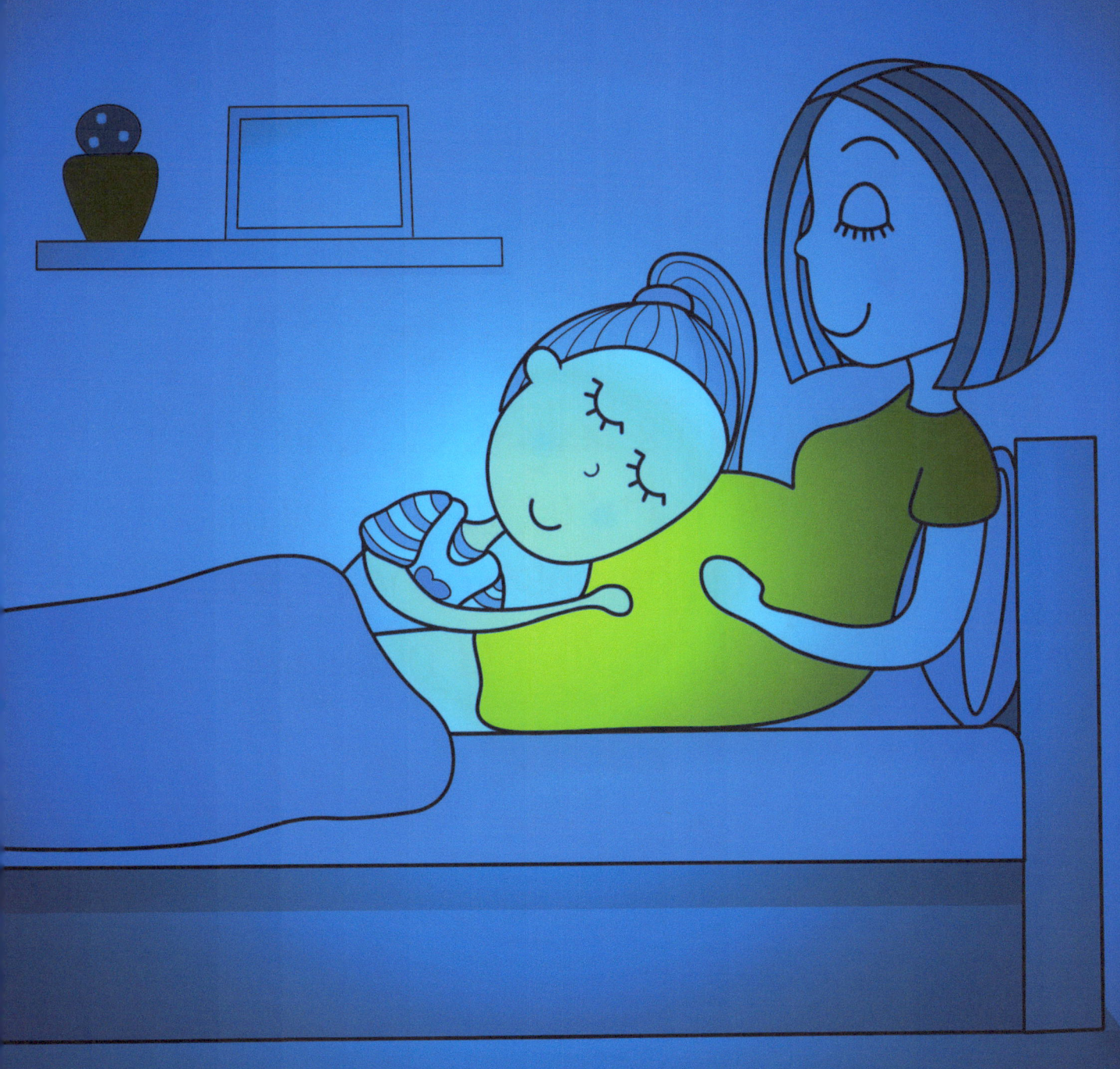

When Mum's belly is big and round,
She will need to give birth.
Baby will be able to look around,
And simply just observe.

Baby will mostly cry, feed and sleep,
It is okay when baby seems sad.
Pat baby softly on the back and feet,
Hold baby's little hand.

You are the older sibling,
So have an important role to play.
Baby will be watching and copying,
Learning from you every day.

So give baby comforting cuddles,
Share all of your toys.
Pick baby up when baby stumbles,
Involve baby in your joys.

Baby's first ultrasound

Place your baby's first ultrasound image here.

Our growing family

Place a photo from your pregnancy photoshoot here.

www.ingramcontent.com/pod-product-compliance
Lightning Source LLC
Chambersburg PA
CBHW041408160426
42811CB00106B/1557